ANIMAL SURVIVAL

WORKING TOGETHER TO SURVIVE

BY LAURA PERDEW

CONTENT CONSULTANT
CHRISTOPHER M. SWAN, PhD
PROFESSOR
DEPT. OF GEOGRAPHY & ENVIRONMENTAL SYSTEMS
UNIVERSITY OF MARYLAND

Kids Core
An Imprint of Abdo Publishing
abdobooks.com

abdobooks.com

Published by Abdo Publishing, a division of ABDO, PO Box 398166, Minneapolis, Minnesota 55439. Copyright © 2023 by Abdo Consulting Group, Inc. International copyrights reserved in all countries. No part of this book may be reproduced in any form without written permission from the publisher. Kids Core™ is a trademark and logo of Abdo Publishing.

Printed in the United States of America, North Mankato, Minnesota.
052022
092022

Cover Photo: Andrey Pavlov/Shutterstock Images
Interior Photos: Vlad Silver/Shutterstock Images, 4–5, 28 (bottom); Fred Olivier/Nature Picture Library/Alamy, 6; Michael Potter/Shutterstock Images, 8; Andrea Izzotti/iStockphoto, 10–11; YG Studio/Shutterstock Images, 13 (dolphins); Shutterstock Images, 13 (background), 19, 25, 26, 29 (top); Narcissa Less/Shutterstock Images, 13 (fish); Ken Griffiths/Shutterstock Images, 14, 28 (top); Mrinal Pal/Shutterstock Images, 16–17; Ray Bulson/Alamy, 20; Trevor Platt/iStockphoto, 22–23, 29 (bottom)

Editor: Ann Schwab
Series Designer: Katharine Hale

Library of Congress Control Number: 2021951725

Publisher's Cataloging-in-Publication Data

Names: Perdew, Laura, author.
Title: Working together to survive / by Laura Perdew
Description: Minneapolis, Minnesota: Abdo Publishing, 2023 | Series: Animal survival | Includes online resources and index.
Identifiers: ISBN 9781532198540 (lib. bdg.) | ISBN 9781644947715 (pbk.) | ISBN 9781098272197 (ebook)
Subjects: LCSH: Animal defenses--Juvenile literature. | Defense measures--Juvenile literature. | Adaptation (Physiology)--Juvenile literature. | Animal behavior--Juvenile literature.
Classification: DDC 591.57--dc23

CONTENTS

Emperor penguins care for their chicks for about five months after they hatch.

CHAPTER 1

PENGUIN HUDDLE

In Antarctica, the temperature is well below freezing. A **colony** of emperor penguins works hard to survive. The males have left to find food. They have not eaten in months. It is the females' turn to care for the newly hatched chicks.

Adult emperor penguins huddle around their chicks to keep them warm.

When the temperature drops more, the females waddle toward each other. They carry their chicks on their feet. To protect the group against the cold and wind, the penguins huddle. They each find a place to tuck in. Each penguin puts its head on the back of the penguin in front of it.

The penguins on the outside of the huddle are hit with the freezing wind. On the inside, it can be as warm as 98 degrees Fahrenheit (37°C)! So, they take turns inside the huddle. Each penguin has a chance to warm up. Working together, the penguins can all stay warm and survive.

Human Teamwork

People can also work together to survive. Families work together to raise children. They share tasks in the home. Adults provide food and shelter. Beyond the home, people also communicate to share information and to take steps to stay safe from danger. This teamwork helps each individual survive.

Female elephants and their young, called calves, live together in groups. All the females in the herd help look after the calves.

Helping Each Other

Like the penguins, many animals work together

in different ways to survive. Some hunt or

gather food together. Others help each other

by warning of danger. The large numbers of animals in herds, colonies, and **schools** help keep individuals safe from predators. Some animals also work together to raise their young. Others build homes such as burrows, hives, and nests. Sometimes animals of different **species** even work together to survive. This is called **mutualism**. No matter the species, working together is a great **adaptation** for survival.

Further Evidence

Look at the website below. Does it give any new evidence to support Chapter One?

Emperor Penguin

abdocorelibrary.com/working -together-to-survive

Bottlenose dolphins are known for their intelligence and problem-solving ability.

CHAPTER 2

SEARCHING FOR FOOD

An important part of animal survival is finding food. In the shallow ocean near Florida, bottlenose dolphins work together to hunt fish. When they detect a school, they move in.

One dolphin swims in a circle around the fish. As it moves, it slaps the seafloor. This creates a mud ring around the fish. The fish think they are trapped. They panic. So they attempt to escape the mud ring by jumping out of the water. Meanwhile, the other dolphins are waiting with their mouths open to catch the jumping fish.

Hunting in Groups

Gray wolves in North America hunt large animals, such as bison. To do this, they hunt together in packs. They circle the herd. Then they close in, hoping to make the bison panic. The goal is to separate one bison from the herd. The wolves work together to capture the prey.

Bottlenose Dolphins' Clever Fishing Trick

2. Fish leap out of the water to escape the mud.

3. Dolphins wait nearby to catch fish.

1. Tail slapping while swimming in a circle stirs up mud.

Bottlenose dolphins work together to hunt for fish. They create a mud circle in the ocean water, causing fish to panic. When the fish jump out of the water to escape the mud, the dolphins are ready to grab them.

Leaf-cutter ants use teamwork to carry a leaf back to the nest.

Growing a Garden

Many species of ants work together to carry food back to their nests. Leaf-cutter ants get their food in a special way. Worker ants from the colony bring leaves back to the nest. But the ants don't eat these leaves. They use them to grow a fungus garden! The fungus is what the ants eat. By working together, these animals have food. This helps all of them survive.

A PBS documentary describes how leaf-cutter ants collect leaves:

> They find their way by following a trail of pheromones, chemical signals left by other ants to mark their path to a good leafy tree and back home again.

Source: "Leaf-Cutter Ants: A Farming Super-Organism." *PBS LearningMedia: Nature*, n.d. pbslearningmedia.org. Accessed 1 Dec. 2021.

Comparing Texts

Think about the quote. Does it support the information in this chapter? Or does it give new information? Explain how in a few sentences.

Meerkats stay safe from predators by living in large groups.

CHAPTER 3

TEAMWORK

In addition to finding food, there are other important ways animals work together. For example, meerkats live in large groups. This helps them stay safe. The adults take turns as guards.

The guard climbs to a high spot to watch for predators. If the guard spots danger, it barks or whistles to the others. Everyone scrambles to a burrow for cover.

Working and Living in Harmony

In honeybee hives, everyone has a job to do. Some worker bees **forage** for good nectar.

Busy Builders

Beaver families work together to stay safe, raise their young, and collect food. They also work together to build dams and lodges. The dams stop the flow of water to create a pond. Then the beavers build the lodge in the pond, where the family is safe from predators.

Honeybees work together to build and maintain the honeycomb.

Others take care of **larvae**. Still other bees build the honeycomb and clean and defend the hive. They also take care of the queen. Her job is to lay the eggs. This teamwork ensures the survival of the whole hive.

A raft of sea otters floats in the ocean near Koniuji Island, Alaska.

Sea otters spend most of their lives in the ocean. They often rest by floating on their backs. But sleeping in the ocean is tricky. The otters will come together in large groups called rafts. Researchers have found up to 1,000 sea otters in a single raft! They wrap themselves in seaweed to stay in place. But they also rely on each other. Sometimes they even hold hands! This keeps them from drifting away from each other. Together they stay safe.

Explore Online

Visit the website below. Does it give any new information about meerkats that wasn't in Chapter Three?

Meerkat

abdocorelibrary.com/working-together-to-survive

Zebras and ostriches help each other avoid predators.

CHAPTER 4

MUTUALISM

Animals that work together don't always belong to the same species. Mutualism benefits both species in the relationship. This makes for some unusual friendships.

Ostriches and zebras are two species that work together. Both are prey for large, fast predators such as lions.

While zebras have great eyesight, ostriches do not. But ostriches have an excellent sense of smell. Zebras do not. The two species sometimes travel together because they warn each other of nearby predators. Together they

Mutualism between Animals and Plants

Mutualism also occurs between animals and plants. Pollination is a great example. In this case, pollinator animals such as bees and butterflies eat from plants. As they move from one plant to another, they spread pollen. This helps the plants reproduce.

Predator fish such as eels allow cleaner wrasses to clean their mouths.

have both good sight and a good sense of smell!

Helpful Friends

In the ocean, cleaner wrasse fish and larger reef fish are another example of mutualism. The cleaner wrasses provide a service to the larger fish. The larger fish come to a cleaning station.

A cleaner wrasse cleans a larger fish's gills.

This is a spot in the ocean where fish and other animals come to get cleaned up. There, the wrasses eat parasites and dead tissue off the other fish. This is a meal for the wrasses. The benefit for the larger fish is that it keeps them clean and healthy. Scientists have discovered that removing the parasites makes the larger fish healthier both physically and mentally. Working together helps animals of all kinds to survive!

Even gray reef sharks visit cleaning stations. A *BBC Earth* documentary states that while other reef fish hide in coral when these sharks appear, the cleaner wrasse does not:

> The cleaner wrasse isn't like the other fish and rushes head on towards this top predator. . . . It removes any leftovers or parasites from the shark's mouth.

Source: "Fearless Fish Cleans Shark's Mouth." *YouTube*, uploaded by BBC Earth, 16 Nov. 2019, youtube.com. Accessed 1 Dec. 2021.

What's the Big Idea?

Read this quote carefully. What is its main idea? Explain how the main idea is supported by details.

SURVIVAL FACTS

Some animals work together to hunt, collect, or grow food.

Other animals may work together to defend against predators, warn against danger, raise their young, or build homes.

For some animals living in large groups, each member has a job.

Sometimes, animals of different species work together, and the relationship helps both animals.

Glossary

adaptation
a trait or behavior that helps an animal or plant survive in its environment

colony
a group of insects that live and work together

forage
to search for food

larvae
the young, wingless forms of many insects that hatch from eggs

mutualism
a close relationship between two different species in which both benefit

school
a group of fish or of another sea creature

species
a group of similar living things that can have young together

Online Resources

To learn more about animals working together to survive, visit our free resource websites below.

Visit **abdocorelibrary.com** or scan this QR code for free Common Core resources for teachers and students, including vetted activities, multimedia, and booklinks, for deeper subject comprehension.

Visit **abdobooklinks.com** or scan this QR code for free additional online weblinks for further learning. These links are routinely monitored and updated to provide the most current information available.

Learn More

Romero, Libby. *Animal Architects.* National Geographic, 2019.

Ventura, Marne. *Busy as a Bee: Are Bees Active?* Abdo, 2022.

Index

About the Author

Laura Perdew is a mom, writing consultant, and author of more than 40 books for children. She writes both fiction and nonfiction with a focus on nature, the environment, and environmental issues. She lives and plays in Boulder, Colorado.